This book i

The Adventures Of
Dylan And Spencer
The Detective Dogs

The Case Of The Walnut Thief

Mathilde Miller

The Green Meadows farm, where Dylan and Spencer, the two detective dogs live, was a patchwork of gold and amber. It was autumn and the days grew shorter, but the excitement of the season filled every moment with a vibrant glow.

One early morning, as the dew was still on the grass, the farm woke to a peculiar sight. The piglets were agitated, gathered around, oinking noisily, their snouts pointing at something in their midst.

A small, empty sack lay in the mud, a sad reminder of what once contained a treasure trove of walnuts. Spencer, the more adventurous of the two, trotted over to have a look at the commotion, his tail wagging.

"Hey, Dylan! Wake up. You've got to come over here!" His eyes sparkled with excitement, searching for clues.

"What's all the fuss about?" Dylan yawned, stretching out his small limbs before deciding to investigate. Spencer showed him the spot where the empty sack with a few walnuts left in it, was lying between the pigs.

"Looks like someone had a midnight snack," Dylan mused, tilting his head to the side as he studied the scene. Dylan's nose twitched as he caught the faint scent of something other than walnuts. "Do you smell that?" he whispered to Spencer.

Spencer took a cautious step forward and sniffed the air. "It's faint, but I think it's leading that way," he murmured, his ears perking up. They both followed the trail, their noses leading them through a maze of possibilities. They weaved through the orchard, the apple trees standing tall and silent, each step bringing them closer to the culprit.

Spencer's ears perked up as he heard the scurrying sound of tiny paws coming from the farms storage barn. Without a word, they both dashed towards the source. The shed door was slightly ajar.

Spencer nudged the door open with his snout and the two dogs crept into the barn. The scent grew stronger, now unmistakable— walnuts and something else, something they hadn't encountered before.

Dylan peered around, his nose quivering with anticipation. "I do smell something," he whispered. The barn was a treasure trove of scents and sounds. They approached the big basket of walnuts that stood proudly on a wooden shelf.

Suddenly, a flash of movement caught Dylan's eye. "Look!" he barked, pointing his paw upwards.

A tiny figure scurried along a wooden beam, walnuts clutched tightly in its mouth. It was a squirrel, its bushy tail flicking with excitement.

Spencer's eyes widened in surprise. "How did a squirrel get in here?" he whispered. They had never seen a squirrel so bold as to venture into the farm's storage. The squirrel chattered back at them, its cheeks puffed out with more walnuts.

"Let's get it!" Spencer exclaimed, his excitement overtaking his fear. He leaped up, his paws trying to catch the squirrel.

Dylan took a step back and prepared to pounce. The squirrel, sensing their intentions, dashed away up to the rafters, running between the wooden beams.

Dylan wove around barrels and crates with surprising grace for his size. The squirrel, nimble and quick, seemed to enjoy the game, pausing to taunt them before darting away again.

Their barks echoed through the barn. The squirrel's path grew more erratic. It was clear that it knew the layout of the barn better than the two pups. They had to be clever if they were going to catch it.

"Spencer, split up," Dylan called. "You go left, I'll go right. We'll meet at the back." Spencer nodded and took off, his paws thumping against the ground.

The squirrel, now cornered, chattered angrily from its perch. Its eyes darted back and forth, searching for an escape. As the dogs neared, the squirrel made its move. It leaped from the shelf, aiming for the open barn door. Dylan lunged, but the squirrel was too fast.

It slipped through the gap between his paws and darted into the daylight. The two pups raced after it, their breath coming in quick pants.

The squirrel sprinted across the farmyard, it was clear that it was heading back to the safety of the forest. As the squirrel approached the edge of the woods, Dylan and Spencer's spirits began to sink. The forest was vast and the squirrel had the advantage of speed and knowledge of the terrain.

"We can't let it get away," Spencer panted, his legs burning from the sprint. "We won't," Dylan assured him, his eyes never leaving the squirrel's retreating figure. "We'll just have to be clever next time."

In the following days, the two detectives put their heads together. They had to outsmart the squirrel. Spencer suggested they set a trap, something that would appeal to its greed, while Dylan thought they should track it down during the night when it would be less alert.

The duo decided to follow the squirrel into the forest, where the squirrel's kin resided. But they would need help, help from a good friend. Luna, the old owl, who lived in the forest and knew everything that went on there.

A few nights later, they were lucky. On their patrol they noticed the farm's storage door was ajar. "Golly," Spencer murmured, "it must have learned how to pick locks. It's a master thief."

They walked closer, their paws making no sound on the hard ground. Inside, they found the squirrel, sniffing on the corn they had layed out as bait for it.

The squirrel, noticing the two dogs, dropped the corn and tried to make a break for it. But Dylan and Spencer were too quick. They herded it out into the open, their barks echoing through the quiet farm. The ginger thief jumped up upon the tractor, then up onto the barn, over the roof, down again and off into the nearby forest.

Dylan and Spencer looked at each other, pleased because, so far, everything had gone according to plan. They set out to follow the thief into the forest where Luna and her friends waited for them. Cleverly positioned, like sentinels, they had a good view over the forest.

They guided the two all the way until they reached a big clearing with a grove in the middle. The dogs approached, their eyes scanning the ground for clues. "You know," Spencer murmured, "this squirrel seems to be smarter than the others." Dylan nodded. "It's like he's got some kind of … I don't know, purpose."

Then, they spotted the squirrel on a small mound in the middle of the grove. Dylan whispered, "What do you think it's doing?" The squirrel had led them on a merry chase, but it was clear that it didn't notice them following it.

A few more steps and they would confront the thief. But what they saw made them stop. Dylan and Spencer shared a surprised look. This was not what they had expected.

As they approached the squirrels' domain, they saw the ginger squirrel, surrounded by a gathering of its kin and lots of other small forest animals. The nuts from the farm were being sorted and distributed among the group. Each creature's eyes shining with relief and gratitude. The ginger squirrel was not stealing the nuts for itself.

It was sharing them with the animals who had suffered from a harsher autumn and whose natural food sources had dwindled. The two dogs, their tails drooping slightly in realization, watched the scene unfold.

The squirrel looked up, noticing their presence. It approached them cautiously and spoke slowly and quietly, but got more confident when it realised the dogs were listening.

The squirrel revealed that a storm had ravaged their usual winter cache, leaving them with no choice but to seek food elsewhere. Dylan and Spencer sat down, understanding how hard it must be to survive in the wilderness.

"I've taken it up as my duty to ensure that all the creatures of the forest would survive the harsh months ahead," the squirrel said. "My name is Robin and I help those in need. Even if that means that I have to take it from the farm. You're so rich. You have plenty and no worries should the winter be long and cold."

Dylan and Spencer shared a look, the gravity of their find sinking in.

They knew what they had to do. "Listen Robin, we are going to help you." Dylan said. "Help me? But how? You don't want to get into any trouble," Robin replied.

"We won't. We'll think of something. We promise to be back soon." Spencer joined in. "But promise, not to steal from the farm anymore, it's wrong. If you carry on stealing, there will nothing that we can do for you."

Robin tilted his head and thought for a moment. "I trust you," he said. "Go back to your farm and let's meet here again after the sun has risen twice. Then you can let me know what your plan is."

The two detectives turned back towards the farm. As they emerged from the forest, the first light of dawn began to break over the horizon. The roosters began to crow, and the cows lowed sleepily in the distance.

Tired and exhausted, they arrived at the farm gate. Deep in thought, the two dogs made their way to the barn. "We have to prepare a speech to the farm community," Dylan said, yawning and gently falling asleep.

The following day, they had a short nap in the hay and a quick breakfast from the farmer, Mr. Green. Lying on the veranda they figured out a plan. When the sun was high in the sky, Dylan and Spencer began their work.

They had to get as many of the farm animals together as possible. "After lunch," Dylan told them, "we're going to have a meeting in the barn. Everybody who can, please come, it's important." Word spread quickly among the farm animals, and after lunch, the barn was filled with chatter and excitement.

"Listen!" Dylan called out, his voice carrying over the rustling of the barn. "We need your help!" The barn went quiet. Dylan and Spencer sat up on a high hay bale, their eyes gleaming with excitement. They had a tale to tell.

"We've found the thief, a squirrel named Robin," Dylan began. "He's been stealing nuts, berries and other things from us. But not because he's greedy or a mere thief. He steels to give to those in need."

The farm animals stared at them, bemusement clear in their expressions. Dylan and Spencer took turns explaining the squirrel's daring raids and his escape tactics. They recounted the squirrel's bravery and his dedication to the less fortunate of the forest.

The farm animals listened with rapt attention, their expressions gradually shifting from scepticism to admiration. "We want to help him," Spencer said, "but we can't do it alone." Dylan and Spencer took turns, explaining the plan to their new allies.

The farm animals huddled closer, their interest piqued. The chickens clucked in agreement, and even the cows stopped their lazy chewing to listen.

"We could give some of our corn," suggested Bessie, the plumpest cow with the most gentlest eyes. "The squirrels can eat that, too." "And I can spare some berries from my patch," added Mrs. Rabbit, who had been quietly listening from the corner of the barn. "The garden's been more than generous this year."

They all looked at each other, a collective determination forming among them.

They had all heard the whispers of hard times in the forest, of animals going hungry and cold. This squirrel's brave deeds resonated deeply with their sense of community and fairness.

"We'll each contribute what we can to the cause," said Old Jack, the farm's donkey, putting down a big carrot, the pigs shuffled over with a few extra apples they had stashed away.

"Here," Mrs. Owl said, dropping some warm feathers at the dogs' paws. "And that's from us," Mrs. Tillie, the big sheep, said, dropping some warm wool onto the pile.

Dylan and Spencer watched with hope and pride. "We'll spread the word," Dylan said. "We'll tell every animal about the squirrel's mission and ask them to donate and give what they can spare."

The next day saw a flurry of activity in the early morning hours. The pile grew larger and the excitement in the barn was palpable. The farm animals whispered about the squirrel's heroics, their tales growing more grandiose and adventurous with each retelling.

The donations grew so plentiful that Old Jack had to go and get one of his baskets, woven from the strongest of straw. "We can't have all this food lying around for the rats to get into," he said with a wink. The animals nodded, knowing that the real reason was to keep their operation hidden.

When the morning of the second day came, it was time to get the bounty to the squirrel into the forest. Dylan and Spencer where just able to carry the basket between them. It was a long way though.

Old Jack couldn't watch them struggle. "Let me do it, boys. You show the way." Together they made their way into the forest.

Robin watched them approach from the safety of a distant branch. His curiosity was piqued by the sight of the two dogs with a donkey in tow.

They approached the meeting point, an ancient oak tree in the grove. The squirrel's eyes narrowed as he saw the big basket on Jack's back. The donkey stepped forward with his precious cargo.

Robin's eyes grew wide. Around him, more squirrels and small creatures of the forest appeared and cautiously approached the trio. Dylan and Spencer looked at each other, their tails wagging in excitement.

They had hoped to gain Robin's trust, but this was more than they had dared to expect. The squirrels, usually so shy and secretive, began to trust them, coming closer to accept their gifts with tiny bows.

Robin had underestimated the loyalty and kindness of the dogs. He had been raised on tales of fierce farm creatures that took what they wanted without care for the lives they disrupted.

But here were Dylan and Spencer, offering friendship and support in their hour of need. Perhaps not all creatures were as self-centred as he had been taught to believe.

He turned to them, a glint of mischief in his eye. "Thank you, Dylan and Spencer and all your friends," Robin chittered, his tiny voice filled with warmth, "Your support is like a warm nut on a cold winter's day."

Followed by Jack, they arrived back on the farm. The other animals couldn't help but notice the change in the two dogs. The farm bustled with excitement. They had all found a new purpose beyond their daily routines.

A few days later, as the sun set in the sky, a frantic shouting and the patter of tiny paws approached them. It was Robin, his eyes wide with terror, his fur ruffled. He skidded to a halt in front of the barn, panting heavily.

"Guy...Guy's gang," he managed to choke out. "They've ... they've found our hoard!" Dylan and Spencer exchanged a puzzled look. "Who?" Spencer's voice was sharp with shock.

The squirrel looked at them, "Guy and his guys...they're the meanest rats in the forest. They're dangerous!" Robin took a shaky breath, "they must have been watching us. They knew where to look and took everything we had stored in the hollow oak."

Dylan and Spencer shared a look of disbelief before springing into action. "We can't let this stand," Dylan barked. "We have to help Robin to get it back."

The squirrel looked at them doubtfully. "You are...going to fight them?" Dylan's tail wagged determinedly. "We can't just sit here while they take what's rightfully yours. We're in this together, Robin."

Spencer nodded, flexing his muscles slightly. "We're not exactly pushovers ourselves, Robin. Besides, we have the element of surprise. They won't be expecting us to come after them."

Robin hesitated and then agreed. "Alright, I'll take you to their cave. But we have to be careful." They set off into the forest, Robin leading the way.

The woods grew denser and the dogs could feel the tension in the air as they approached the clearing where the rats lived. "Their cave is over there, just behind the tree with the beehive," Robin whispered, his eyes darting around nervously. "But we have to be quiet. They're always having lookouts."

Dylan and Spencer nodded in understanding. They had heard stories of the notorious rat gang, but seeing the fear in Robin's eyes made it all too real.

They knew that brute force would not be enough to take on these seasoned thieves. They had to be clever.

As they approached the clearing, they could hear the distant echoes of raucous laughter and the clinking of stolen goods. The cave's entrance was guarded by two burly rats with beady eyes and snarling mouths. Dylan's ears perked up, listening to their taunts and jeers. He smiled; an idea began to form in his mind.

"I have an idea. Do you remember that beehive we found last summer?" Spencer grined, "and the crow that tried to steal their honey?" "Exactly," Dylan murmured, "we'll need to be careful, but maybe we can get the guards to leave their post. Robin, you go and collect some berries. Spencer, you search for the perfect rock to serve as a projectile." After a few moments, Spencer found one and brought it over. "This one should have enough weight to make a convincing thud against the tree trunk," Spencer said.

"Here, Robin," Dylan whispered, ponting to the rock. "When I say go, you throw this at the tree near the hive, that should get their attention."

Robin took the rock, feeling the weight of their plan in his paws. "Got it," he murmured, passing them the berries which they carefully arranged into a trail leading from the beehive to the rats' cave. It was a risky move. "Ready?" Spencer whispered, his eyes locked onto Dylan's. Dylan nodded to Robin, "Go!"

With a swift motion, Robin threw the rock. It hit the tree trunk with a smack, echoing through the forest. The two rats at the cave entrance jumped in surprise, their eyes darting around to find the source of the disturbance.

The rats spotted the shiny red berries and their snouts twitched greedily. One took a tentative step forward, then another, following the trail that led away from the safety of the cave.

"Now, Robin," Spencer hissed. The squirrel nodded and with a quick dart, he shot up the nearest tree. The dogs watched as he leaped from branch to branch, impressed by his agility. In moments, he had reached the beehive, his tiny paws flicking it just enough to stir the bees' anger a bit more, without knocking it down.

The rats, now fully engrossed in their pursuit of the berries, didn't notice the growing buzz above them. The bees grew more agitated. Spencer held his breath as Robin gave the hive one final nudge. It swayed ominously before a single bee took flight, zig-zagging through the air. The rats froze, their greed turning to terror as more bees took to the air, their flight pattern erratic.

The two rats, soon surrounded by a cloud of enraged bees, bolted back towards the cave. The bees, mistaking the rats for the culprits of the disturbance, gave chase. Dylan and Spencer watched as the two rats squealed and ducked, swiping at the stinging cloud with their tails. They dived into the cave, seeking refuge from the furious swarm.

But the bees, driven by instinct and anger, did not relent. They followed the culprits into the dark, narrow space, buzzing angrily. Chaos erupted in the cave as all the rats tried to get out, squeaking.

Dylan and Spencer watched. Their eyes wide with a mix of horror and amusement.

The plan was working. One rat after the other was coming out of the cave. First of all came Guy, the meanest rat in the forest, followed by the rest of his gang, screaming and swearing. They disappeared into the forest in all directions. The bees had done their part, and now it was time for the real heist to begin.

As the last of the rats disappeared into the darkness, the dogs couldn't help but chuckle at the chaos. Robin, unable to contain his glee, rolled onto his back and held his tummy, his laughter a series of high-pitched squeaks.

The bees, their mission accomplished, retreated back to their hive, buzzing angrily but leaving the trio untouched.

"The lair is empty. Let's go," Spencer murmured, his eyes gleaming with excitement. The inside was a mess, with stolen goods scattered everywhere, nuts, seeds, and shiny trinkets littered the floor. It was clear that the rats had been hoarding for a long time. "This will last us all winter," Robin said.

He turned to Dylan and Spencer, his eyes gleaming with gratitude.

"Thank you," he said, his voice quivering with emotion. "Without your bravery and cunning, we never would have done this." Dylan and Spencer exchanged a proud look, their chests puffed out slightly.

"We couldn't have done it without you, Robin," Spencer said, nudging the squirrel with his nose. "Indeed," Dylan added, a grin splitting his muzzle.

"You're the real hero here. Now, let's go and find a new hiding place, get all this out and go back to the farm before the rats understand what hit 'em."

On their way back, they could still hear Robin's laughter echoing through the trees. They looked at each other and, despite being so tired, couldn't help but smile.

The thought of those panicking rats, their tiny paws scurrying in the dark, was just too much. It had been a risky plan, but, in the end, they had secured the hoard.

Tired but happy, they left the forest, knowing that their new friends would be just fine.

Back on the farm, the days grew shorter and the nights grew colder as winter approached. The farm prepared for the harsh season, and the detective duo continued to keep a watchful eye on the forest, ensuring that no other creature would dare to threaten their newfound friends.

One crisp morning, as the first snowflakes began to fall, Dylan and Spencer heard screams which sent a shiver down their spines. Loud Baaa's and Maaa's pierced the stillness of the early morning.

Following the sound, they found the farm's herd of goats huddled together, their eyes wide with alarm. The snow around them was stained dark red.

The two detective dogs shared a look; a new adventure lay ahead of them. Let the chase begin.

The Case Of:

The Missing Eggs

The Walnut Thief

The Golden Rudd

... and more to come.
Check them out on AMAZON !

Did you know ...

... That squirrels can jump 12 feet (app. 2,65 m) and more?

They are rodents and love nuts, fruits and seeds. They spend about 15 hours a day sleeping and you can find them all over the world, except in the Antarctica and Australia.

There are more than 200 different species. There are flying squirrels, ground squirrels and tree squirrels. Most of them prefer to be active at dusk and dawn. In the summer, the tree squirrels love the sun and may remain out of their nest all day long. There are red squirrel tones, which go from a bright ginger to a quiet dark colour; sometimes they are grey or almost black.

Squirrels are small animals and at birth, their chances to survive aren't very high. If they make it to adulthood though, they can grow 4-6 years old; the oldest one recorded was 12 years old.

When they are born, they are naked and blind. The mother suckles them every three or four hours for several weeks. After about seven weeks, they'll open their eyes and after 10 weeks, their teeth are fully grown. They can start eating solid food and follow their mother out into the branches.

Their natural enemies are pine martens, foxes, coyotes, snakes and birds of prey, like hawks.

Printed in Poland
by Amazon Fulfillment
Poland Sp. z o.o., Wrocław

48032489R00029